Phantasmagoria
And
Other Poems

By
Charles Dodgson,
AKA - Lewis Carroll

Double 9
BOOKS

Phantasmagoria And Other Poems

by Charles Dodgson, AKA - Lewis Carroll

ISBN: 978-93-56562-73-8

Published by

DOUBLE 9 BOOKS

2/13-B, Ansari Road
Daryaganj, New Delhi - 110002
info@double9books.com
www.double9books.com
Tel. 011-40042856

Printed in India.

About the Author

Lewis carroll became born charles lutwidge dodgson on january 27, 1832, in daresbury, cheshire, england. The son of a clergyman, carroll. From a completely early age he entertained himself and his own family by means of appearing magic tricks and marionette indicates, and via writing poetry for his selfmade newspapers. In 1846 he entered rugby college, and in 1854 he graduated from christ church college, oxford. He turned into a hit in his look at of arithmetic and writing, and remained at the college after commencement to educate.

He on the whole wrote comedian fantasies and funny verse that changed into regularly very childlike. Carroll published his novel alice's adventures in wonderland in 1865, accompanied by using through the searching glass in 1872. Alice's story started as a piece of extemporaneous whimsy meant to entertain 3 little women on a boating ride in 1862. Both of these works were taken into consideration children's novels that had been satirical in nature and in exemplification of carroll's wit.

Contents

PHANTASMAGORIA

CANTO I:

The Trystyng

One winter night, at half-past nine, Cold, tired, and cross, and muddy, I had come home, too late to dine, And supper, with cigars and wine, Was waiting in the study.

There was a strangeness in the room, And Something white and wavy Was standing near me in the gloom - I took it for the carpet-broom Left by that careless slavey.

But presently the Thing began To shiver and to sneeze: On which I said "Come, come, my man! That's a most inconsiderate plan. Less noise there, if you please!"

"I've caught a cold," the Thing replies, "Out there upon the landing." I turned to look in some surprise, And there, before my very eyes, A little Ghost was standing!

He trembled when he caught my eye, And got behind a chair. "How came you here," I said, "and why? I never saw a thing so shy. Come out! Don't shiver there!"

He said "I'd gladly tell you how, And also tell you why; But" (here he gave a little bow) "You're in so bad a temper now, You'd think it all a lie.

"And as to being in a fright, Allow me to remark That Ghosts have just as good a right In every way, to fear the light, As Men to fear the dark."

"No plea," said I, "can well excuse Such cowardice in you: For Ghosts can visit when they choose, Whereas we Humans ca'n't refuse To grant the interview."

He said "A flutter of alarm Is not unnatural, is it? I really feared you meant some harm: But, now I see that you are calm, Let me explain my visit.

"Houses are classed, I beg to state, According to the number Of Ghosts that they accommodate: (The Tenant merely counts as WEIGHT, With Coals and other lumber).

"This is a 'one-ghost' house, and you When you arrived last summer, May have remarked a Spectre who Was doing all that Ghosts can do To welcome the new-comer.

"In Villas this is always done - However cheaply rented: For, though of course there's less of fun When there is only room for one, Ghosts have to be contented.

"That Spectre left you on the Third - Since then you've not been haunted: For, as he never sent us word, 'Twas quite by accident we heard That any one was wanted.

"A Spectre has first choice, by right, In filling up a vacancy; Then Phantom, Goblin, Elf, and Sprite - If all these fail them, they invite The nicest Ghoul that they can see.

"The Spectres said the place was low, And that you kept bad wine: So, as a Phantom had to go, And I was first, of course, you know, I couldn't well decline."

"No doubt," said I, "they settled who Was fittest to be sent Yet still to choose a brat like you, To haunt a man of forty-two, Was no great compliment!"

"I'm not so young, Sir," he replied, "As you might think. The fact is, In caverns by the water-side, And other places that I've tried, I've had a lot of practice:

"But I have never taken yet A strict domestic part, And in my flurry I forget The Five Good Rules of Etiquette We have to know by heart."

My sympathies were warming fast Towards the little fellow: He was so utterly aghast At having found a Man at last, And looked so scared and yellow.

"At least," I said, "I'm glad to find A Ghost is not a DUMB thing! But pray sit down: you'll feel inclined (If, like myself, you have not dined) To take a snack of something:

"Though, certainly, you don't appear A thing to offer FOOD to! And then I shall be glad to hear - If you will say them loud and clear - The Rules that you allude to."

"Thanks! You shall hear them by and by. This IS a piece of luck!" "What may I offer you?" said I. "Well, since you ARE so kind, I'll try A little bit of duck.

"ONE slice! And may I ask you for Another drop of gravy?" I sat and looked at him in awe, For certainly I never saw A thing so white and wavy.

And still he seemed to grow more white, More vapoury, and wavier - Seen in the dim and flickering light, As he proceeded to recite His "Maxims of Behaviour."

CANTO II:

Hys Fyve Rules

"My First--but don't suppose," he said, "I'm setting you a riddle - Is--if your Victim be in bed, Don't touch the curtains at his head, But take them in the middle,

"And wave them slowly in and out, While drawing them asunder; And in a minute's time, no doubt, He'll raise his head and look about With eyes of wrath and wonder.

"And here you must on no pretence Make the first observation. Wait for the Victim to commence: No Ghost of any common sense Begins a conversation.

"If he should say 'HOW CAME YOU HERE?' (The way that YOU began, Sir,) In such a case your course is clear - 'ON THE BAT'S BACK, MY LITTLE DEAR!' Is the appropriate answer.

"If after this he says no more, You'd best perhaps curtail your Exertions--go and shake the door, And then, if he begins to snore, You'll know the thing's a failure.

"By day, if he should be alone - At home or on a walk - You merely give a hollow groan, To indicate the kind of tone In which you mean to talk.

"But if you find him with his friends, The thing is rather harder. In such a case success depends On picking up some candle-ends, Or butter, in the larder.

"With this you make a kind of slide (It answers best with suet), On which you must contrive to glide, And swing yourself from side to side - One soon learns how to do it.

"The Second tells us what is right In ceremonious calls:- 'FIRST BURN A BLUE OR CRIMSON LIGHT' (A thing I quite forgot to-night), 'THEN SCRATCH THE DOOR OR WALLS.'"

I said "You'll visit HERE no more, If you attempt the Guy. I'll have no bonfires on MY floor - And, as for scratching at the door, I'd like to see you try!"

"The Third was written to protect The interests of the Victim, And tells us, as I recollect, TO TREAT HIM WITH A GRAVE RESPECT, AND NOT TO CONTRADICT HIM."

"That's plain," said I, "as Tare and Tret, To any comprehension: I only wish SOME Ghosts I've met Would not so CONSTANTLY forget The maxim that you mention!"

"Perhaps," he said, "YOU first transgressed The laws of hospitality: All Ghosts instinctively detest The Man that fails to treat his guest With proper cordiality.

"If you address a Ghost as 'Thing!' Or strike him with a hatchet, He is permitted by the King To drop all FORMAL parleying - And then you're SURE to catch it!

"The Fourth prohibits trespassing Where other Ghosts are quartered: And those convicted of the thing (Unless when pardoned by the King) Must instantly be slaughtered.

"That simply means 'be cut up small': Ghosts soon unite anew. The process scarcely hurts at all - Not more than when YOU're what you call 'Cut up' by a Review.

"The Fifth is one you may prefer That I should quote entire:- THE KING MUST BE ADDRESSED AS 'SIR.' THIS, FROM A SIMPLE COURTIER, IS ALL THE LAWS REQUIRE:

"BUT, SHOULD YOU WISH TO DO THE THING WITH OUT-AND-OUT POLITENESS, ACCOST HIM AS 'MY GOBLIN KING! AND ALWAYS USE, IN ANSWERING, THE PHRASE 'YOUR ROYAL WHITENESS!'

"I'm getting rather hoarse, I fear, After so much reciting : So, if you don't object, my dear, We'll try a glass of bitter beer - I think it looks inviting."

CANTO III:

Scarmoges

"And did you really walk," said I, "On such a wretched night? I always fancied Ghosts could fly - If not exactly in the sky, Yet at a fairish height."

"It's very well," said he, "for Kings To soar above the earth: But Phantoms often find that wings - Like many other pleasant things - Cost more than they are worth.

"Spectres of course are rich, and so Can buy them from the Elves: But WE prefer to keep below - They're stupid company, you know, For any but themselves:

"For, though they claim to be exempt From pride, they treat a Phantom As something quite beneath contempt - Just as no Turkey ever dreamt Of noticing a Bantam."

"They seem too proud," said I, "to go To houses such as mine. Pray, how did they contrive to know So quickly that 'the place was low,' And that I 'kept bad wine'?"

"Inspector Kobold came to you--" The little Ghost began. Here I broke in--"Inspector who? Inspecting Ghosts is something new! Explain yourself, my man!"

"His name is Kobold," said my guest: "One of the Spectre order: You'll very often see him dressed In a yellow gown, a crimson vest, And a night-cap with a border.

"He tried the Brocken business first, But caught a sort of chill ; So came to England to be nursed, And here it took the form of THIRST, Which he complains of still.

"Port-wine, he says, when rich and sound, Warms his old bones like nectar: And as the inns, where it is found, Are his especial hunting-ground, We call him the INN-SPECTRE."

I bore it--bore it like a man - This agonizing witticism! And nothing could be sweeter than My temper, till the Ghost began Some most provoking criticism.

"Cooks need not be indulged in waste; Yet still you'd better teach them Dishes should have SOME SORT of taste. Pray, why are all the cruets placed Where nobody can reach them?

"That man of yours will never earn His living as a waiter! Is that queer THING supposed to burn? (It's far too dismal a concern To call a Moderator).

"The duck was tender, but the peas Were very much too old: And just remember, if you please, The NEXT time you have toasted cheese, Don't let them send it cold.

"You'd find the bread improved, I think, By getting better flour: And have you anything to drink That looks a LITTLE less like ink, And isn't QUITE so sour?"

Then, peering round with curious eyes, He muttered "Goodness gracious!" And so went on to criticise - "Your room's an inconvenient size: It's neither snug nor spacious.

"That narrow window, I expect, Serves but to let the dusk in--" "But please," said I, "to recollect 'Twas fashioned by an architect Who pinned his faith on Ruskin!"

"I don't care who he was, Sir, or On whom he pinned his faith! Constructed by whatever law, So poor a job I never saw, As I'm a living Wraith!

"What a re-markable cigar! How much are they a dozen?" I growled "No matter what they are! You're getting as familiar As if you were my cousin!

"Now that's a thing I WILL NOT STAND, And so I tell you flat." "Aha," said he, "we're getting grand!" (Taking a bottle in his hand) "I'll soon arrange for THAT!"

And here he took a careful aim, And gaily cried "Here goes!" I tried to dodge it as it came, But somehow caught it, all the same, Exactly on my nose.

And I remember nothing more That I can clearly fix, Till I was sitting on the floor, Repeating "Two and five are four, But FIVE AND TWO are six."

What really passed I never learned, Nor guessed: I only know That, when at last my sense returned, The lamp, neglected, dimly burned - The fire was getting low -

Through driving mists I seemed to see A Thing that smirked and smiled: And found that he was giving me A lesson in Biography, As if I were a child.

CANTO IV:

Hys Nouryture

"Oh, when I was a little Ghost, A merry time had we! Each seated on his favourite post, We chumped and chawed the buttered toast They gave us for our tea."

"That story is in print!" I cried. "Don't say it's not, because It's known as well as Bradshaw's Guide!" (The Ghost uneasily replied He hardly thought it was).

"It's not in Nursery Rhymes? And yet I almost think it is - 'Three little Ghosteses' were set 'On posteses,' you know, and ate Their 'buttered toasteses.'

"I have the book; so if you doubt it--" I turned to search the shelf. "Don't stir!" he cried. "We'll do without it: I now remember all about it; I wrote the thing myself.

"It came out in a 'Monthly,' or At least my agent said it did: Some literary swell, who saw It, thought it seemed adapted for The Magazine he edited.

"My father was a Brownie, Sir; My mother was a Fairy. The notion had occurred to her, The children would be happier, If they were taught to vary.

"The notion soon became a craze; And, when it once began, she Brought us all out in different ways - One was a Pixy, two were Fays, Another was a Banshee;

"The Fetch and Kelpie went to school And gave a lot of trouble; Next came a Poltergeist and Ghoul, And then two Trolls (which broke the rule), A Goblin, and a Double -

"(If that's a snuff-box on the shelf," He added with a yawn, "I'll take a pinch)--next came an Elf, And then a Phantom (that's myself), And last, a Leprechaun.

"One day, some Spectres chanced to call, Dressed in the usual white: I stood and watched them in the hall, And couldn't make them out at all, They seemed so strange a sight.

"I wondered what on earth they were, That looked all head and sack; But Mother told me not to stare, And then she twitched me by the hair, And punched me in the back.

"Since then I've often wished that I Had been a Spectre born. But what's the use?" (He heaved a sigh.) "THEY are the ghost-nobility, And look on US with scorn.

"My phantom-life was soon begun: When I was barely six, I went out with an older one - And just at first I thought it fun, And learned a lot of tricks.

"I've haunted dungeons, castles, towers - Wherever I was sent: I've often sat and howled for hours, Drenched to the skin with driving showers, Upon a battlement.

"It's quite old-fashioned now to groan When you begin to speak: This is the newest thing in tone--" And here (it chilled me to the bone) He gave an AWFUL squeak.

"Perhaps," he added, "to YOUR ear That sounds an easy thing? Try it yourself, my little dear! It took ME something like a year, With constant practising.

"And when you've learned to squeak, my man, And caught the double sob, You're pretty much where you began: Just try and gibber if you can! That's something LIKE a job!

"I'VE tried it, and can only say I'm sure you couldn't do it, e- ven if you practised night and day, Unless you have a turn that way, And natural ingenuity.

"Shakspeare I think it is who treats Of Ghosts, in days of old, Who 'gibbered in the Roman streets,' Dressed, if you recollect, in sheets - They must have found it cold.

"I've often spent ten pounds on stuff, In dressing as a Double; But, though it answers as a puff, It never has effect enough To make it worth the trouble.

"Long bills soon quenched the little thirst I had for being funny. The setting-up is always worst: Such heaps of things you want at first, One must be made of money!

"For instance, take a Haunted Tower, With skull, cross-bones, and sheet; Blue lights to burn (say) two an hour, Condensing lens of extra power, And set of chains complete:

"What with the things you have to hire - The fitting on the robe - And testing all the coloured fire - The outfit of itself would tire The patience of a Job!

"And then they're so fastidious, The Haunted-House Committee: I've often known them make a fuss Because a Ghost was French, or Russ, Or even from the City!

"Some dialects are objected to - For one, the IRISH brogue is: And then, for all you have to do, One pound a week they offer you, And find yourself in Bogies!

CANTO V:

Byckerment

"Don't they consult the 'Victims,' though?" I said. "They should, by rights, Give them a chance--because, you know, The tastes of people differ so, Especially in Sprites."

The Phantom shook his head and smiled. "Consult them? Not a bit! 'Twould be a job to drive one wild, To satisfy one single child - There'd be no end to it!"

"Of course you can't leave CHILDREN free," Said I, "to pick and choose: But, in the case of men like me, I think 'Mine Host' might fairly be Allowed to state his views."

He said "It really wouldn't pay - Folk are so full of fancies. We visit for a single day, And whether then we go, or stay, Depends on circumstances.

"And, though we don't consult 'Mine Host' Before the thing's arranged, Still, if he often quits his post, Or is not a well-mannered Ghost, Then you can have him changed.

"But if the host's a man like you - I mean a man of sense; And if the house is not too new--" "Why, what has THAT," said I, "to do With Ghost's convenience?"

"A new house does not suit, you know - It's such a job to trim it: But, after twenty years or so, The wainscotings begin to go, So twenty is the limit."

"To trim" was not a phrase I could Remember having heard: "Perhaps," I said, "you'll be so good As tell me what is understood Exactly by that word?"

"It means the loosening all the doors," The Ghost replied, and laughed: "It means the drilling holes by scores In all the skirting-boards and floors, To make a thorough draught.

"You'll sometimes find that one or two Are all you really need To let the wind come whistling through - But HERE there'll be a lot to do!" I faintly gasped "Indeed!

"If I'd been rather later, I'll Be bound," I added, trying (Most unsuccessfully) to smile, "You'd have been busy all this while, Trimming and beautifying?"

"Why, no," said he; "perhaps I should Have stayed another minute - But still no Ghost, that's any good, Without an introduction would Have ventured to begin it.

"The proper thing, as you were late, Was certainly to go: But, with the roads in such a state, I got the Knight-Mayor's leave to wait For half an hour or so."

"Who's the Knight-Mayor?" I cried. Instead Of answering my question, "Well, if you don't know THAT," he said, "Either you never go to bed, Or you've a grand digestion!

"He goes about and sits on folk That eat too much at night: His duties are to pinch, and poke, And squeeze them till they nearly choke." (I said "It serves them right!")

"And folk who sup on things like these--" He muttered, "eggs and bacon - Lobster--and duck--and toasted cheese - If they don't get an awful squeeze, I'm very much mistaken!

"He is immensely fat, and so Well suits the occupation: In point of fact, if you must know, We used to call him years ago, THE MAYOR AND CORPORATION!

"The day he was elected Mayor I KNOW that every Sprite meant To vote for ME, but did not dare - He was so frantic with despair And furious with excitement.

"When it was over, for a whim, He ran to tell the King; And being the reverse of slim, A two-mile trot was not for him A very easy thing.

"So, to reward him for his run (As it was baking hot, And he was over twenty stone), The King proceeded, half in fun, To knight him on the spot."

"'Twas a great liberty to take!" (I fired up like a rocket). "He did it just for punning's sake: 'The man,' says Johnson, 'that would make A pun, would pick a pocket!'"

"A man," said he, "is not a King." I argued for a while, And did my best to prove the thing - The Phantom merely listening With a contemptuous smile.

At last, when, breath and patience spent, I had recourse to smoking - "Your AIM," he said, "is excellent: But--when you call it ARGUMENT - Of course you're only joking?"

Stung by his cold and snaky eye, I roused myself at length To say "At least I do defy The veriest sceptic to deny That union is strength!"

"That's true enough," said he, "yet stay--" I listened in all meekness - "UNION is strength, I'm bound to say; In fact, the thing's as clear as day; But ONIONS are a weakness."

CANTO VI:

Dyscomfyture

As one who strives a hill to climb, Who never climbed before: Who finds it, in a little time, Grow every moment less sublime, And votes the thing a bore:

Yet, having once begun to try, Dares not desert his quest, But, climbing, ever keeps his eye On one small hut against the sky Wherein he hopes to rest:

Who climbs till nerve and force are spent, With many a puff and pant: Who still, as rises the ascent, In language grows more violent, Although in breath more scant:

Who, climbing, gains at length the place That crowns the upward track. And, entering with unsteady pace, Receives a buffet in the face That lands him on his back:

And feels himself, like one in sleep, Glide swiftly down again, A helpless weight, from steep to steep, Till, with a headlong giddy sweep, He drops upon the plain -

So I, that had resolved to bring Conviction to a ghost, And found it quite a different thing From any human arguing, Yet dared not quit my post

But, keeping still the end in view To which I hoped to come, I strove to prove the matter true By putting everything I knew Into an axiom:

Commencing every single phrase With 'therefore' or 'because,' I blindly reeled, a hundred ways, About the syllogistic maze, Unconscious where I was.

Quoth he "That's regular clap-trap: Don't bluster any more. Now DO be cool and take a nap! Such a ridiculous old chap Was never seen before!

"You're like a man I used to meet, Who got one day so furious In arguing, the simple heat Scorched both his slippers off his feet!" I said "THAT'S VERY CURIOUS!"

"Well, it IS curious, I agree, And sounds perhaps like fibs: But still it's true as true can be - As sure as your name's Tibbs," said he. I said "My name's NOT Tibbs."

"NOT Tibbs!" he cried--his tone became A shade or two less hearty - "Why, no," said I. "My proper name Is Tibbets--" "Tibbets?" "Aye, the same." "Why, then YOU'RE NOT THE PARTY!"

With that he struck the board a blow That shivered half the glasses. "Why couldn't you have told me so Three quarters of an hour ago, You prince of all the asses?

"To walk four miles through mud and rain, To spend the night in smoking, And then to find that it's in vain - And I've to do it all again - It's really TOO provoking!

"Don't talk!" he cried, as I began To mutter some excuse. "Who can have patience with a man That's got no more discretion than An idiotic goose?

"To keep me waiting here, instead Of telling me at once That this was not the house!" he said. "There, that'll do--be off to bed! Don't gape like that, you dunce!"

"It's very fine to throw the blame On ME in such a fashion! Why didn't you enquire my name The very minute that you came?" I answered in a passion.

"Of course it worries you a bit To come so far on foot - But how was I to blame for it?" "Well, well!" said he. "I must admit That isn't badly put.

"And certainly you've given me The best of wine and victual - Excuse my violence," said he, "But accidents like this, you see, They put one out a little.

"'Twas MY fault after all, I find - Shake hands, old Turnip-top!" The name was hardly to my mind, But, as no doubt he meant it kind, I let the matter drop.

"Good-night, old Turnip-top, good-night! When I am gone, perhaps They'll send you some inferior Sprite, Who'll keep you in a constant fright And spoil your soundest naps.

"Tell him you'll stand no sort of trick; Then, if he leers and chuckles, You just be handy with a stick (Mind that it's pretty hard and thick) And rap him on the knuckles!

"Then carelessly remark 'Old coon! Perhaps you're not aware That, if you don't behave, you'll soon Be chuckling to another tune - And so you'd best take care!'

"That's the right way to cure a Sprite Of such like goings-on - But gracious me! It's getting light! Good-night, old Turnip-top, good-night!" A nod, and he was gone.

CANTO VII:

Sad Souvenaunce

"What's this?" I pondered. "Have I slept? Or can I have been drinking?" But soon a gentler feeling crept Upon me, and I sat and wept An hour or so, like winking.

"No need for Bones to hurry so!" I sobbed. "In fact, I doubt If it was worth his while to go - And who is Tibbs, I'd like to know, To make such work about?

"If Tibbs is anything like me, It's POSSIBLE," I said, "He won't be over-pleased to be Dropped in upon at half-past three, After he's snug in bed.

"And if Bones plagues him anyhow - Squeaking and all the rest of it, As he was doing here just now - I prophesy there'll be a row, And Tibbs will have the best of it!"

Then, as my tears could never bring The friendly Phantom back, It seemed to me the proper thing To mix another glass, and sing The following Coronach.

'AND ART THOU GONE, BELOVED GHOST? BEST OF FAMILIARS! NAY THEN, FAREWELL, MY DUCKLING ROAST, FAREWELL, FAREWELL, MY TEA AND TOAST, MY MEERSCHAUM AND CIGARS!

THE HUES OF LIFE ARE DULL AND GRAY, THE SWEETS OF LIFE INSIPID, WHEN thou, MY CHARMER, ART AWAY - OLD BRICK, OR RATHER, LET ME SAY, OLD PARALLELEPIPED!'

Instead of singing Verse the Third, I ceased--abruptly, rather: But, after such a splendid word I felt that it would be absurd To try it any farther.

So with a yawn I went my way To seek the welcome downy, And slept, and dreamed till break of day Of Poltergeist and Fetch and Fay And Leprechaun and Brownie!

For year I've not been visited By any kind of Sprite; Yet still they echo in my head, Those parting words, so kindly said, "Old Turnip-top, good-night!"

———

Phantasmagoria And Other Poems

ECHOES

L ady Clara Vere de Vere Was eight years old, she said: Every ringlet, lightly shaken, ran itself in golden thread.

She took her little porringer: Of me she shall not win renown: For the baseness of its nature shall have strength to drag her down.

"Sisters and brothers, little Maid? There stands the Inspector at thy door: Like a dog, he hunts for boys who know not two and two are four."

"Kind words are more than coronets," She said, and wondering looked at me: "It is the dead unhappy night, and I must hurry home to tea."

A SEA DIRGE

There are certain things--as, a spider, a ghost, The income-tax, gout, an umbrella for three - That I hate, but the thing that I hate the most Is a thing they call the Sea.

Pour some salt water over the floor - Ugly I'm sure you'll allow it to be: Suppose it extended a mile or more, THAT'S very like the Sea.

Beat a dog till it howls outright - Cruel, but all very well for a spree: Suppose that he did so day and night, THAT would be like the Sea.

I had a vision of nursery-maids; Tens of thousands passed by me - All leading children with wooden spades, And this was by the Sea.

Who invented those spades of wood? Who was it cut them out of the tree? None, I think, but an idiot could - Or one that loved the Sea.

It is pleasant and dreamy, no doubt, to float With 'thoughts as boundless, and souls as free': But, suppose you are very unwell in the boat, How do you like the Sea?

There is an insect that people avoid (Whence is derived the verb 'to flee'). Where have you been by it most annoyed? In lodgings by the Sea.

If you like your coffee with sand for dregs, A decided hint of salt in your tea, And a fishy taste in the very eggs - By all means choose the Sea.

And if, with these dainties to drink and eat, You prefer not a vestige of grass or tree, And a chronic state of wet in your feet, Then--I recommend the Sea.

For I have friends who dwell by the coast - Pleasant friends they are to me! It is when I am with them I wonder most That anyone likes the Sea.

They take me a walk: though tired and stiff, To climb the heights I madly agree; And, after a tumble or so from the cliff, They kindly suggest the Sea.

I try the rocks, and I think it cool That they laugh with such an excess of glee, As I heavily slip into every pool That skirts the cold cold Sea.

Ye Carpette Knyghte

I have a horse--a ryghte good horse - Ne doe Y envye those Who scoure ye playne yn headye course Tyll soddayne on theyre nose They lyghte wyth unexpected force Yt ys--a horse of clothes.

I have a saddel--"Say'st thou soe? Wyth styrruppes, Knyghte, to boote?" I sayde not that--I answere "Noe" - Yt lacketh such, I woote: Yt ys a mutton-saddel, loe! Parte of ye fleecye brute.

I have a bytte--a ryghte good bytte - As shall bee seene yn tyme. Ye jawe of horse yt wyll not fytte; Yts use ys more sublyme. Fayre Syr, how deemest thou of yt? Yt ys--thys bytte of rhyme.

HIAWATHA'S PHOTOGRAPHING

[I n an age of imitation, I can claim no special merit for this slight attempt at doing what is known to be so easy. Any fairly practised writer, with the slightest ear for rhythm, could compose, for hours together, in the easy running metre of 'The Song of Hiawatha.' Having, then, distinctly stated that I challenge no attention in the following little poem to its merely verbal jingle, I must beg the candid reader to confine his criticism to its treatment of the subject.]

From his shoulder Hiawatha Took the camera of rosewood, Made of sliding, folding rosewood; Neatly put it all together. In its case it lay compactly, Folded into nearly nothing;

But he opened out the hinges, Pushed and pulled the joints and hinges, Till it looked all squares and oblongs, Like a complicated figure In the Second Book of Euclid.

This he perched upon a tripod - Crouched beneath its dusky cover - Stretched his hand, enforcing silence - Said, "Be motionless, I beg you!" Mystic, awful was the process.

All the family in order Sat before him for their pictures: Each in turn, as he was taken, Volunteered his own suggestions, His ingenious suggestions.

First the Governor, the Father: He suggested velvet curtains Looped about a massy pillar; And the corner of a table, Of a rosewood dining-table. He would hold a scroll of something, Hold it firmly in his left-hand; He would keep his right-hand buried (Like Napoleon) in his waistcoat; He would contemplate the distance With a look of pensive meaning, As of ducks that die ill tempests.

Grand, heroic was the notion: Yet the picture failed entirely: Failed, because he moved a little, Moved, because he couldn't help it.

Next, his better half took courage; SHE would have her picture taken. She came dressed beyond description, Dressed in jewels and in satin Far too gorgeous for an empress. Gracefully she sat down

---

sideways, With a simper scarcely human, Holding in her hand a bouquet Rather larger than a cabbage. All the while that she was sitting, Still the lady chattered, chattered, Like a monkey in the forest. "Am I sitting still?" she asked him. "Is my face enough in profile? Shall I hold the bouquet higher? Will it came into the picture?" And the picture failed completely.

Next the Son, the Stunning-Cantab: He suggested curves of beauty, Curves pervading all his figure, Which the eye might follow onward, Till they centered in the breast-pin, Centered in the golden breast-pin. He had learnt it all from Ruskin (Author of 'The Stones of Venice,' 'Seven Lamps of Architecture,' 'Modern Painters,' and some others); And perhaps he had not fully Understood his author's meaning; But, whatever was the reason, All was fruitless, as the picture Ended in an utter failure.

Next to him the eldest daughter: She suggested very little, Only asked if he would take her With her look of 'passive beauty.'

Her idea of passive beauty Was a squinting of the left-eye, Was a drooping of the right-eye, Was a smile that went up sideways To the corner of the nostrils.

Hiawatha, when she asked him, Took no notice of the question, Looked as if he hadn't heard it; But, when pointedly appealed to, Smiled in his peculiar manner, Coughed and said it 'didn't matter,' Bit his lip and changed the subject.

Nor in this was he mistaken, As the picture failed completely.

So in turn the other sisters.

Last, the youngest son was taken: Very rough and thick his hair was, Very round and red his face was, Very dusty was his jacket, Very fidgety his manner. And his overbearing sisters Called him names he disapproved of: Called him Johnny, 'Daddy's Darling,' Called him Jacky, 'Scrubby School-boy.' And, so awful was the picture, In comparison the others Seemed, to one's bewildered fancy, To have partially succeeded.

Finally my Hiawatha Tumbled all the tribe together, ('Grouped' is not the right expression), And, as happy chance would have it Did at last obtain a picture Where the faces all succeeded: Each came out a perfect likeness.

Then they joined and all abused it, Unrestrainedly abused it, As the worst and ugliest picture They could possibly have dreamed of. 'Giving one such strange expressions - Sullen, stupid, pert expressions. Really any one would take us (Any one that did not know us) For the most unpleasant people!' (Hiawatha seemed to think so, Seemed to think it not unlikely). All together rang their voices, Angry, loud, discordant voices, As of dogs that howl in concert, As of cats that wail in chorus.

But my Hiawatha's patience, His politeness and his patience, Unaccountably had vanished, And he left that happy party. Neither did he leave them slowly, With the calm deliberation, The intense deliberation Of a photographic artist: But he left them in a hurry, Left them in a mighty hurry, Stating that he would not stand it, Stating in emphatic language What he'd be before he'd stand it. Hurriedly he packed his boxes: Hurriedly the porter trundled On a barrow all his boxes: Hurriedly he took his ticket: Hurriedly the train received him: Thus departed Hiawatha.

MELANCHOLETTA

With saddest music all day long She soothed her secret sorrow: At night she sighed "I fear 'twas wrong Such cheerful words to borrow. Dearest, a sweeter, sadder song I'll sing to thee to-morrow."

I thanked her, but I could not say That I was glad to hear it: I left the house at break of day, And did not venture near it Till time, I hoped, had worn away Her grief, for nought could cheer it!

My dismal sister! Couldst thou know The wretched home thou keepest! Thy brother, drowned in daily woe, Is thankful when thou sleepest; For if I laugh, however low, When thou'rt awake, thou weepest!

I took my sister t'other day (Excuse the slang expression) To Sadler's Wells to see the play In hopes the new impression Might in her thoughts, from grave to gay Effect some slight digression.

I asked three gay young dogs from town To join us in our folly, Whose mirth, I thought, might serve to drown My sister's melancholy: The lively Jones, the sportive Brown, And Robinson the jolly.

The maid announced the meal in tones That I myself had taught her, Meant to allay my sister's moans Like oil on troubled water: I rushed to Jones, the lively Jones, And begged him to escort her.

Vainly he strove, with ready wit, To joke about the weather - To ventilate the last 'ON DIT' - To quote the price of leather - She groaned "Here I and Sorrow sit: Let us lament together!"

I urged "You're wasting time, you know: Delay will spoil the venison." "My heart is wasted with my woe! There is no rest--in Venice, on The Bridge of Sighs!" she quoted low From Byron and from Tennyson.

I need not tell of soup and fish In solemn silence swallowed, The sobs that ushered in each dish, And its departure followed, Nor yet my suicidal wish To BE the cheese I hollowed.

Some desperate attempts were made To start a conversation; "Madam," the sportive Brown essayed, "Which kind of recreation, Hunting or fishing, have you made Your special occupation?"

Her lips curved downwards instantly, As if of india-rubber. "Hounds IN FULL CRY I like," said she: (Oh how I longed to snub her!) "Of fish, a whale's the one for me, IT IS SO FULL OF BLUBBER!"

The night's performance was "King John." "It's dull," she wept, "and so-so!" Awhile I let her tears flow on, She said they soothed her woe so! At length the curtain rose upon 'Bombastes Furioso.'

In vain we roared; in vain we tried To rouse her into laughter: Her pensive glances wandered wide From orchestra to rafter - "TIER UPON TIER!" she said, and sighed; And silence followed after.

A VALENTINE

[Sent to a friend who had complained that I was glad enough to see him when he came, but didn't seem to miss him if he stayed away.]

And cannot pleasures, while they last, Be actual unless, when past, They leave us shuddering and aghast, With anguish smarting? And cannot friends be firm and fast, And yet bear parting?

And must I then, at Friendship's call, Calmly resign the little all (Trifling, I grant, it is and small) I have of gladness, And lend my being to the thrall Of gloom and sadness?

And think you that I should be dumb, And full dolorum omnium, Excepting when YOU choose to come And share my dinner? At other times be sour and glum And daily thinner?

Must he then only live to weep, Who'd prove his friendship true and deep By day a lonely shadow creep, At night-time languish, Oft raising in his broken sleep The moan of anguish?

The lover, if for certain days His fair one be denied his gaze, Sinks not in grief and wild amaze, But, wiser wooer, He spends the time in writing lays, And posts them to her.

And if the verse flow free and fast, Till even the poet is aghast, A touching Valentine at last The post shall carry, When thirteen days are gone and past Of February.

Farewell, dear friend, and when we meet, In desert waste or crowded street, Perhaps before this week shall fleet, Perhaps to-morrow. I trust to find YOUR heart the seat Of wasting sorrow.

THE THREE VOICES

The First Voice

He trilled a carol fresh and free, He laughed aloud for very glee: There came a breeze from off the sea:

It passed athwart the glooming flat - It fanned his forehead as he sat - It lightly bore away his hat,

All to the feet of one who stood Like maid enchanted in a wood, Frowning as darkly as she could.

With huge umbrella, lank and brown, Unerringly she pinned it down, Right through the centre of the crown.

Then, with an aspect cold and grim, Regardless of its battered rim, She took it up and gave it him.

A while like one in dreams he stood, Then faltered forth his gratitude In words just short of being rude:

For it had lost its shape and shine, And it had cost him four-and-nine, And he was going out to dine.

"To dine!" she sneered in acid tone. "To bend thy being to a bone Clothed in a radiance not its own!"

The tear-drop trickled to his chin: There was a meaning in her grin That made him feel on fire within.

"Term it not 'radiance,'" said he: "'Tis solid nutriment to me. Dinner is Dinner: Tea is Tea."

And she "Yea so? Yet wherefore cease? Let thy scant knowledge find increase. Say 'Men are Men, and Geese are Geese.'"

He moaned: he knew not what to say. The thought "That I could get away!" Strove with the thought "But I must stay.

"To dine!" she shrieked in dragon-wrath. "To swallow wines all foam and froth! To simper at a table-cloth!

"Say, can thy noble spirit stoop To join the gormandising troup Who find a solace in the soup?

"Canst thou desire or pie or puff? Thy well-bred manners were enough, Without such gross material stuff."

"Yet well-bred men," he faintly said, "Are not willing to be fed: Nor are they well without the bread."

Her visage scorched him ere she spoke: "There are," she said, "a kind of folk Who have no horror of a joke.

"Such wretches live: they take their share Of common earth and common air: We come across them here and there:

"We grant them--there is no escape - A sort of semi-human shape Suggestive of the man-like Ape."

"In all such theories," said he, "One fixed exception there must be. That is, the Present Company."

Baffled, she gave a wolfish bark: He, aiming blindly in the dark, With random shaft had pierced the mark.

She felt that her defeat was plain, Yet madly strove with might and main To get the upper hand again.

Fixing her eyes upon the beach, As though unconscious of his speech, She said "Each gives to more than each."

He could not answer yea or nay: He faltered "Gifts may pass away." Yet knew not what he meant to say.

"If that be so," she straight replied, "Each heart with each doth coincide. What boots it? For the world is wide."

"The world is but a Thought," said he: "The vast unfathomable sea Is but a Notion--unto me."

And darkly fell her answer dread Upon his unresisting head, Like half a hundredweight of lead.

"The Good and Great must ever shun That reckless and abandoned one Who stoops to perpetrate a pun.

"The man that smokes--that reads the Times - That goes to Christmas Pantomimes - Is capable of ANY crimes!"

He felt it was his turn to speak, And, with a shamed and crimson cheek, Moaned "This is harder than Bezique!"

But when she asked him "Wherefore so?" He felt his very whiskers glow, And frankly owned "I do not know."

While, like broad waves of golden grain, Or sunlit hues on cloistered pane, His colour came and went again.

Pitying his obvious distress, Yet with a tinge of bitterness, She said "The More exceeds the Less."

"A truth of such undoubted weight," He urged, "and so extreme in date, It were superfluous to state."

Roused into sudden passion, she In tone of cold malignity: "To others, yea: but not to thee."

But when she saw him quail and quake, And when he urged "For pity's sake!" Once more in gentle tones she spake.

"Thought in the mind doth still abide That is by Intellect supplied, And within that Idea doth hide:

"And he, that yearns the truth to know, Still further inwardly may go, And find Idea from Notion flow:

"And thus the chain, that sages sought, Is to a glorious circle wrought, For Notion hath its source in Thought."

So passed they on with even pace: Yet gradually one might trace A shadow growing on his face.

The Second Voice

They walked beside the wave-worn beach; Her tongue was very apt to teach, And now and then he did beseech

She would abate her dulcet tone, Because the talk was all her own, And he was dull as any drone.

She urged "No cheese is made of chalk": And ceaseless flowed her dreary talk, Tuned to the footfall of a walk.

Her voice was very full and rich, And, when at length she asked him "Which?" It mounted to its highest pitch.

He a bewildered answer gave, Drowned in the sullen moaning wave, Lost in the echoes of the cave.

He answered her he knew not what: Like shaft from bow at random shot, He spoke, but she regarded not.

She waited not for his reply, But with a downward leaden eye Went on as if he were not by

Sound argument and grave defence, Strange questions raised on "Why?" and "Whence?" And wildly tangled evidence.

When he, with racked and whirling brain, Feebly implored her to explain, She simply said it all again.

Wrenched with an agony intense, He spake, neglecting Sound and Sense, And careless of all consequence:

"Mind--I believe--is Essence--Ent - Abstract--that is--an Accident - Which we--that is to say--I meant--"

When, with quick breath and cheeks all flushed, At length his speech was somewhat hushed, She looked at him, and he was crushed.

It needed not her calm reply: She fixed him with a stony eye, And he could neither fight nor fly.

While she dissected, word by word, His speech, half guessed at and half heard, As might a cat a little bird.

Then, having wholly overthrown His views, and stripped them to the bone, Proceeded to unfold her own.

"Shall Man be Man? And shall he miss Of other thoughts no thought but this, Harmonious dews of sober bliss?

"What boots it? Shall his fevered eye Through towering nothingness descry The grisly phantom hurry by?

"And hear dumb shrieks that fill the air; See mouths that gape, and eyes that stare And redden in the dusky glare?

"The meadows breathing amber light, The darkness toppling from the height, The feathery train of granite Night?

"Shall he, grown gray among his peers, Through the thick curtain of his tears Catch glimpses of his earlier years,

"And hear the sounds he knew of yore, Old shufflings on the sanded floor, Old knuckles tapping at the door?

"Yet still before him as he flies One pallid form shall ever rise, And, bodying forth in glassy eyes

"The vision of a vanished good, Low peering through the tangled wood, Shall freeze the current of his blood."

Still from each fact, with skill uncouth And savage rapture, like a tooth She wrenched some slow reluctant truth.

Till, like a silent water-mill, When summer suns have dried the rill, She reached a full stop, and was still.

Dead calm succeeded to the fuss, As when the loaded omnibus Has reached the railway terminus:

When, for the tumult of the street, Is heard the engine's stifled beat, The velvet tread of porters' feet.

With glance that ever sought the ground, She moved her lips without a sound, And every now and then she frowned.

He gazed upon the sleeping sea, And joyed in its tranquillity, And in that silence dead, but she

To muse a little space did seem, Then, like the echo of a dream, Harked back upon her threadbare theme.

Still an attentive ear he lent But could not fathom what she meant: She was not deep, nor eloquent.

He marked the ripple on the sand: The even swaying of her hand Was all that he could understand.

He saw in dreams a drawing-room, Where thirteen wretches sat in gloom, Waiting--he thought he knew for whom:

He saw them drooping here and there, Each feebly huddled on a chair, In attitudes of blank despair:

Oysters were not more mute than they, For all their brains were pumped away, And they had nothing more to say -

Save one, who groaned "Three hours are gone!" Who shrieked "We'll wait no longer, John! Tell them to set the dinner on!"

The vision passed: the ghosts were fled: He saw once more that woman dread: He heard once more the words she said.

He left her, and he turned aside: He sat and watched the coming tide Across the shores so newly dried.

He wondered at the waters clear, The breeze that whispered in his ear, The billows heaving far and near,

And why he had so long preferred To hang upon her every word: "In truth," he said, "it was absurd."

The Third Voice

Not long this transport held its place: Within a little moment's space Quick tears were raining down his face

His heart stood still, aghast with fear; A wordless voice, nor far nor near, He seemed to hear and not to hear.

"Tears kindle not the doubtful spark. If so, why not? Of this remark The bearings are profoundly dark."

"Her speech," he said, "hath caused this pain. Easier I count it to explain The jargon of the howling main,

"Or, stretched beside some babbling brook, To con, with inexpressive look, An unintelligible book."

Low spake the voice within his head, In words imagined more than said, Soundless as ghost's intended tread:

"If thou art duller than before, Why quittedst thou the voice of lore? Why not endure, expecting more?"

"Rather than that," he groaned aghast, "I'd writhe in depths of cavern vast, Some loathly vampire's rich repast."

"'Twere hard," it answered, "themes immense To coop within the narrow fence That rings THY scant intelligence."

"Not so," he urged, "nor once alone: But there was something in her tone That chilled me to the very bone.

"Her style was anything but clear, And most unpleasantly severe; Her epithets were very queer.

"And yet, so grand were her replies, I could not choose but deem her wise; I did not dare to criticise;

"Nor did I leave her, till she went So deep in tangled argument That all my powers of thought were spent."

A little whisper inly slid, "Yet truth is truth: you know you did." A little wink beneath the lid.

And, sickened with excess of dread, Prone to the dust he bent his head, And lay like one three-quarters dead

The whisper left him--like a breeze Lost in the depths of leafy trees - Left him by no means at his ease.

Once more he weltered in despair, With hands, through denser-matted hair, More tightly clenched than then they were.

When, bathed in Dawn of living red, Majestic frowned the mountain head, "Tell me my fault," was all he said.

When, at high Noon, the blazing sky Scorched in his head each haggard eye, Then keenest rose his weary cry.

And when at Eve the unpitying sun Smiled grimly on the solemn fun, "Alack," he sighed, "what HAVE I done?"

But saddest, darkest was the sight, When the cold grasp of leaden Night Dashed him to earth, and held him tight.

Tortured, unaided, and alone, Thunders were silence to his groan, Bagpipes sweet music to its tone:

"What? Ever thus, in dismal round, Shall Pain and Mystery profound Pursue me like a sleepless hound,

"With crimson-dashed and eager jaws, Me, still in ignorance of the cause, Unknowing what I broke of laws?"

The whisper to his ear did seem Like echoed flow of silent stream, Or shadow of forgotten dream,

The whisper trembling in the wind: "Her fate with thine was intertwined," So spake it in his inner mind:

"Each orbed on each a baleful star: Each proved the other's blight and bar: Each unto each were best, most far:

"Yea, each to each was worse than foe: Thou, a scared dullard, gibbering low, AND SHE, AN AVALANCHE OF WOE!"

TEMA CON VARIAZIONI

[W]hy is it that Poetry has never yet been subjected to that process of Dilution which has proved so advantageous to her sister-art Music? The Diluter gives us first a few notes of some well-known Air, then a dozen bars of his own, then a few more notes of the Air, and so on alternately: thus saving the listener, if not from all risk of recognising the melody at all, at least from the too- exciting transports which it might produce in a more concentrated form. The process is termed "setting" by Composers, and any one, that has ever experienced the emotion of being unexpectedly set down in a heap of mortar, will recognise the truthfulness of this happy phrase.

For truly, just as the genuine Epicure lingers lovingly over a morsel of supreme Venison--whose every fibre seems to murmur "Excelsior!"--yet swallows, ere returning to the toothsome dainty, great mouthfuls of oatmeal-porridge and winkles: and just as the perfect Connoisseur in Claret permits himself but one delicate sip, and then tosses off a pint or more of boarding-school beer: so also -

I never loved a dear Gazelle - NOR ANYTHING THAT COST ME MUCH: HIGH PRICES PROFIT THOSE WHO SELL, BUT WHY SHOULD I BE FOND OF SUCH?

To glad me with his soft black eye MY SON COMES TROTTING HOME FROM SCHOOL; HE'S HAD A FIGHT BUT CAN'T TELL WHY - HE ALWAYS WAS A LITTLE FOOL!

But, when he came to know me well, HE KICKED ME OUT, HER TESTY SIRE: AND WHEN I STAINED MY HAIR, THAT BELLE MIGHT NOTE THE CHANGE, AND THUS ADMIRE

And love me, it was sure to dye A MUDDY GREEN OR STARING BLUE: WHILST ONE MIGHT TRACE, WITH HALF AN EYE, THE STILL TRIUMPHANT CARROT THROUGH.

A GAME OF FIVES

Five little girls, of Five, Four, Three, Two, One: Rolling on the hearthrug, full of tricks and fun.

Five rosy girls, in years from Ten to Six: Sitting down to lessons--no more time for tricks.

Five growing girls, from Fifteen to Eleven: Music, Drawing, Languages, and food enough for seven!

Five winsome girls, from Twenty to Sixteen: Each young man that calls, I say "Now tell me which you MEAN!"

Five dashing girls, the youngest Twenty-one: But, if nobody proposes, what is there to be done?

Five showy girls--but Thirty is an age When girls may be ENGAGING, but they somehow don't ENGAGE.

Five dressy girls, of Thirty-one or more: So gracious to the shy young men they snubbed so much before!

* * * *

Five passe girls--Their age? Well, never mind! We jog along together, like the rest of human kind: But the quondam "careless bachelor" begins to think he knows The answer to that ancient problem "how the money goes"!

POETA FIT, NON NASCITUR

" How shall I be a poet? How shall I write in rhyme? You told me once 'the very wish Partook of the sublime.' Then tell me how! Don't put me off With your 'another time'!"

The old man smiled to see him, To hear his sudden sally; He liked the lad to speak his mind Enthusiastically; And thought "There's no hum-drum in him, Nor any shilly-shally."

"And would you be a poet Before you've been to school? Ah, well! I hardly thought you So absolute a fool. First learn to be spasmodic - A very simple rule.

"For first you write a sentence, And then you chop it small; Then mix the bits, and sort them out Just as they chance to fall: The order of the phrases makes No difference at all.

'Then, if you'd be impressive, Remember what I say, That abstract qualities begin With capitals alway: The True, the Good, the Beautiful - Those are the things that pay!

"Next, when you are describing A shape, or sound, or tint; Don't state the matter plainly, But put it in a hint; And learn to look at all things With a sort of mental squint."

"For instance, if I wished, Sir, Of mutton-pies to tell, Should I say 'dreams of fleecy flocks Pent in a wheaten cell'?" "Why, yes," the old man said: "that phrase Would answer very well.

"Then fourthly, there are epithets That suit with any word - As well as Harvey's Reading Sauce With fish, or flesh, or bird - Of these, 'wild,' 'lonely,' 'weary,' 'strange,' Are much to be preferred."

"And will it do, O will it do To take them in a lump - As 'the wild man went his weary way To a strange and lonely pump'?" "Nay, nay! You must not hastily To such conclusions jump.

"Such epithets, like pepper, Give zest to what you write; And, if you strew them sparely, They whet the appetite: But if you lay them on too thick, You spoil the matter quite!

"Last, as to the arrangement: Your reader, you should show him, Must take what information he Can get, and look for no im- mature disclosure of the drift And purpose of your poem.

"Therefore, to test his patience - How much he can endure - Mention no places, names, or dates, And evermore be sure Throughout the poem to be found Consistently obscure.

"First fix upon the limit To which it shall extend: Then fill it up with 'Padding' (Beg some of any friend): Your great SENSATION-STANZA You place towards the end."

"And what is a Sensation, Grandfather, tell me, pray? I think I never heard the word So used before to-day: Be kind enough to mention one 'Exempli gratia.'"

And the old man, looking sadly Across the garden-lawn, Where here and there a dew-drop Yet glittered in the dawn, Said "Go to the Adelphi, And see the 'Colleen Bawn.'

'The word is due to Boucicault - The theory is his, Where Life becomes a Spasm, And History a Whiz: If that is not Sensation, I don't know what it is.

"Now try your hand, ere Fancy Have lost its present glow--" "And then," his grandson added, "We'll publish it, you know: Green cloth-- gold-lettered at the back - In duodecimo!"

Then proudly smiled that old man To see the eager lad Rush madly for his pen and ink And for his blotting-pad - But, when he thought of PUBLISHING, His face grew stern and sad.

SIZE AND TEARS

When on the sandy shore I sit, Beside the salt sea-wave, And fall into a weeping fit Because I dare not shave - A little whisper at my ear Enquires the reason of my fear.

I answer "If that ruffian Jones Should recognise me here, He'd bellow out my name in tones Offensive to the ear: He chaffs me so on being stout (A thing that always puts me out)."

Ah me! I see him on the cliff! Farewell, farewell to hope, If he should look this way, and if He's got his telescope! To whatsoever place I flee, My odious rival follows me!

For every night, and everywhere, I meet him out at dinner; And when I've found some charming fair, And vowed to die or win her, The wretch (he's thin and I am stout) Is sure to come and cut me out!

The girls (just like them!) all agree To praise J. Jones, Esquire: I ask them what on earth they see About him to admire? They cry "He is so sleek and slim, It's quite a treat to look at him!"

They vanish in tobacco smoke, Those visionary maids - I feel a sharp and sudden poke Between the shoulder-blades - "Why, Brown, my boy! Your growing stout!" (I told you he would find me out!)

"My growth is not YOUR business, Sir!" "No more it is, my boy! But if it's YOURS, as I infer, Why, Brown, I give you joy! A man, whose business prospers so, Is just the sort of man to know!

"It's hardly safe, though, talking here - I'd best get out of reach: For such a weight as yours, I fear, Must shortly sink the beach!" - Insult me thus because I'm stout! I vow I'll go and call him out!

ATALANTA IN CAMDEN-TOWN

Ay, 'twas here, on this spot, In that summer of yore, Atalanta did not Vote my presence a bore, Nor reply to my tenderest talk "She had heard all that nonsense before."

She'd the brooch I had bought And the necklace and sash on, And her heart, as I thought, Was alive to my passion; And she'd done up her hair in the style that the Empress had brought into fashion.

I had been to the play With my pearl of a Peri - But, for all I could say, She declared she was weary, That "the place was so crowded and hot, and she couldn't abide that Dundreary."

Then I thought "Lucky boy! 'Tis for YOU that she whimpers!" And I noted with joy Those sensational simpers: And I said "This is scrumptious!"--a phrase I had learned from the Devonshire shrimpers.

And I vowed "'Twill be said I'm a fortunate fellow, When the breakfast is spread, When the topers are mellow, When the foam of the bride-cake is white, and the fierce orange-blossoms are yellow!"

O that languishing yawn! O those eloquent eyes! I was drunk with the dawn Of a splendid surmise - I was stung by a look, I was slain by a tear, by a tempest of sighs.

Then I whispered "I see The sweet secret thou keepest. And the yearning for ME That thou wistfully weepest! And the question is 'License or Banns?', though undoubtedly Banns are the cheapest."

"Be my Hero," said I, "And let ME be Leander!" But I lost her reply - Something ending with "gander" - For the omnibus rattled so loud that no mortal could quite understand her.

THE LANG COORTIN'

The ladye she stood at her lattice high, Wi' her doggie at her feet; Thorough the lattice she can spy The passers in the street,

"There's one that standeth at the door, And tirleth at the pin: Now speak and say, my popinjay, If I sall let him in."

Then up and spake the popinjay That flew abune her head: "Gae let him in that tirls the pin: He cometh thee to wed."

O when he cam' the parlour in, A woeful man was he! "And dinna ye ken your lover agen, Sae well that loveth thee?"

"And how wad I ken ye loved me, Sir, That have been sae lang away? And how wad I ken ye loved me, Sir? Ye never telled me sae."

Said--"Ladye dear," and the salt, salt tear Cam' rinnin' doon his cheek, "I have sent the tokens of my love This many and many a week.

"O didna ye get the rings, Ladye, The rings o' the gowd sae fine? I wot that I have sent to thee Four score, four score and nine."

"They cam' to me," said that fair ladye. "Wow, they were flimsie things!" Said--"that chain o' gowd, my doggie to howd, It is made o' thae self-same rings."

"And didna ye get the locks, the locks, The locks o' my ain black hair, Whilk I sent by post, whilk I sent by box, Whilk I sent by the carrier?"

"They cam' to me," said that fair ladye; "And I prithee send nae mair!" Said--"that cushion sae red, for my doggie's head, It is stuffed wi' thae locks o' hair."

"And didna ye get the letter, Ladye, Tied wi' a silken string, Whilk I sent to thee frae the far countrie, A message of love to bring?"

"It cam' to me frae the far countrie Wi' its silken string and a'; But it wasna prepaid," said that high-born maid, "Sae I gar'd them tak' it awa'."

"O ever alack that ye sent it back, It was written sae clerkly and well! Now the message it brought, and the boon that it sought, I must even say it mysel'."

Then up and spake the popinjay, Sae wisely counselled he. "Now say it in the proper way: Gae doon upon thy knee!"

The lover he turned baith red and pale, Went doon upon his knee: "O Ladye, hear the waesome tale That must be told to thee!

"For five lang years, and five lang years, I coorted thee by looks; By nods and winks, by smiles and tears, As I had read in books.

"For ten lang years, O weary hours! I coorted thee by signs; By sending game, by sending flowers, By sending Valentines.

"For five lang years, and five lang years, I have dwelt in the far countrie, Till that thy mind should be inclined Mair tenderly to me.

"Now thirty years are gane and past, I am come frae a foreign land: I am come to tell thee my love at last - O Ladye, gie me thy hand!"

The ladye she turned not pale nor red, But she smiled a pitiful smile: "Sic' a coortin' as yours, my man," she said "Takes a lang and a weary while!"

And out and laughed the popinjay, A laugh of bitter scorn: "A coortin' done in sic' a way, It ought not to be borne!"

Wi' that the doggie barked aloud, And up and doon he ran, And tugged and strained his chain o' gowd, All for to bite the man.

"O hush thee, gentle popinjay! O hush thee, doggie dear! There is a word I fain wad say, It needeth he should hear!"

Aye louder screamed that ladye fair To drown her doggie's bark: Ever the lover shouted mair To make that ladye hark:

Shrill and more shrill the popinjay Upraised his angry squall: I trow the doggie's voice that day Was louder than them all!

The serving-men and serving-maids Sat by the kitchen fire: They heard sic' a din the parlour within As made them much admire.

Out spake the boy in buttons (I ween he wasna thin), "Now wha will tae the parlour gae, And stay this deadlie din?"

And they have taen a kerchief, Casted their kevils in, For wha will tae the parlour gae, And stay that deadlie din.

When on that boy the kevil fell To stay the fearsome noise, "Gae in," they cried, "whate'er betide, Thou prince of button-boys!"

Syne, he has taen a supple cane To swinge that dog sae fat: The doggie yowled, the doggie howled The louder aye for that.

Syne, he has taen a mutton-bane - The doggie ceased his noise, And followed doon the kitchen stair That prince of button-boys!

Then sadly spake that ladye fair, Wi' a frown upon her brow: "O dearer to me is my sma' doggie Than a dozen sic' as thou!

"Nae use, nae use for sighs and tears: Nae use at all to fret: Sin' ye've bided sae well for thirty years, Ye may bide a wee langer yet!"

Sadly, sadly he crossed the floor And tirled at the pin: Sadly went he through the door Where sadly he cam' in.

"O gin I had a popinjay To fly abune my head, To tell me what I ought to say, I had by this been wed.

"O gin I find anither ladye," He said wi' sighs and tears, "I wot my coortin' sall not be Anither thirty years

"For gin I find a ladye gay, Exactly to my taste, I'll pop the question, aye or nay, In twenty years at maist."

FOUR RIDDLES

[These consist of two Double Acrostics and two Charades.

No. I. was written at the request of some young friends, who had gone to a ball at an Oxford Commemoration--and also as a specimen of what might be done by making the Double Acrostic A CONNECTED POEM instead of what it has hitherto been, a string of disjointed stanzas, on every conceivable subject, and about as interesting to read straight through as a page of a Cyclopaedia. The first two stanzas describe the two main words, and each subsequent stanza one of the cross "lights."

No. II. was written after seeing Miss Ellen Terry perform in the play of "Hamlet." In this case the first stanza describes the two main words.

No. III. was written after seeing Miss Marion Terry perform in Mr. Gilbert's play of "Pygmalion and Galatea." The three stanzas respectively describe "My First," "My Second," and "My Whole."]

I

There was an ancient City, stricken down With a strange frenzy, and for many a day They paced from morn to eve the crowded town, And danced the night away.

I asked the cause: the aged man grew sad: They pointed to a building gray and tall, And hoarsely answered "Step inside, my lad, And then you'll see it all."

* * * *

Yet what are all such gaieties to me Whose thoughts are full of indices and surds?

$$x^*x \ 7x \ 53 = 11/3$$

But something whispered "It will soon be done: Bands cannot always play, nor ladies smile: Endure with patience the distasteful fun For just a little while!"

A change came o'er my Vision--it was night: We clove a pathway through a frantic throng: The steeds, wild-plunging, filled us with affright: The chariots whirled along.

Within a marble hall a river ran - A living tide, half muslin and half cloth: And here one mourned a broken wreath or fan, Yet swallowed down her wrath;

And here one offered to a thirsty fair (His words half-drowned amid those thunders tuneful) Some frozen viand (there were many there), A tooth-ache in each spoonful.

There comes a happy pause, for human strength Will not endure to dance without cessation; And every one must reach the point at length Of absolute prostration.

At such a moment ladies learn to give, To partners who would urge them over-much, A flat and yet decided negative - Photographers love such.

There comes a welcome summons--hope revives, And fading eyes grow bright, and pulses quicken: Incessant pop the corks, and busy knives Dispense the tongue and chicken.

Flushed with new life, the crowd flows back again: And all is tangled talk and mazy motion - Much like a waving field of golden grain, Or a tempestuous ocean.

And thus they give the time, that Nature meant For peaceful sleep and meditative snores, To ceaseless din and mindless merriment And waste of shoes and floors.

And One (we name him not) that flies the flowers, That dreads the dances, and that shuns the salads, They doom to pass in solitude the hours, Writing acrostic-ballads.

How late it grows! The hour is surely past That should have warned us with its double knock? The twilight wanes, and morning comes at last - "Oh, Uncle, what's o'clock?"

The Uncle gravely nods, and wisely winks. It MAY mean much, but how is one to know? He opens his mouth--yet out of it, methinks, No words of wisdom flow.

II

Empress of Art, for thee I twine This wreath with all too slender skill. Forgive my Muse each halting line, And for the deed accept the will!

* * * *

O day of tears! Whence comes this spectre grim, Parting, like Death's cold river, souls that love? Is not he bound to thee, as thou to him, By vows, unwhispered here, yet heard above?

And still it lives, that keen and heavenward flame, Lives in his eye, and trembles in his tone: And these wild words of fury but proclaim A heart that beats for thee, for thee alone!

But all is lost: that mighty mind o'erthrown, Like sweet bells jangled, piteous sight to see! "Doubt that the stars are fire," so runs his moan, "Doubt Truth herself, but not my love for thee!"

A sadder vision yet: thine aged sire Shaming his hoary locks with treacherous wile! And dost thou now doubt Truth to be a liar? And wilt thou die, that hast forgot to smile?

Nay, get thee hence! Leave all thy winsome ways And the faint fragrance of thy scattered flowers: In holy silence wait the appointed days, And weep away the leaden-footed hours.

III.

The air is bright with hues of light And rich with laughter and with singing: Young hearts beat high in ecstasy, And banners wave, and bells are ringing: But silence falls with fading day, And there's an end to mirth and play. Ah, well-a-day

Rest your old bones, ye wrinkled crones! The kettle sings, the firelight dances. Deep be it quaffed, the magic draught That fills the soul with golden fancies! For Youth and Pleasance will not stay, And ye are withered, worn, and gray. Ah, well-a-day!

O fair cold face! O form of grace, For human passion madly yearning! O weary air of dumb despair, From marble won, to marble turning! "Leave us not thus!" we fondly pray. "We cannot let thee pass away!" Ah, well-a-day!

IV.

My First is singular at best: More plural is my Second: My Third is far the pluralest - So plural-plural, I protest It scarcely can be reckoned!

My First is followed by a bird: My Second by believers In magic art: my simple Third Follows, too often, hopes absurd And plausible deceivers.

My First to get at wisdom tries - A failure melancholy! My Second men revered as wise: My Third from heights of wisdom flies To depths of frantic folly.

My First is ageing day by day: My Second's age is ended: My Third enjoys an age, they say, That never seems to fade away, Through centuries extended.

My Whole? I need a poet's pen To paint her myriad phases: The monarch, and the slave, of men - A mountain-summit, and a den Of dark and deadly mazes -

A flashing light--a fleeting shade - Beginning, end, and middle Of all that human art hath made Or wit devised! Go, seek HER aid, If you would read my riddle!

FAME'S PENNY-TRUMPET

[A ffectionately dedicated to all "original researchers" who pant for "endowment."]

Blow, blow your trumpets till they crack, Ye little men of little souls! And bid them huddle at your back - Gold-sucking leeches, shoals on shoals!

Fill all the air with hungry wails - "Reward us, ere we think or write! Without your Gold mere Knowledge fails To sate the swinish appetite!"

And, where great Plato paced serene, Or Newton paused with wistful eye, Rush to the chace with hoofs unclean And Babel-clamour of the sty

Be yours the pay: be theirs the praise: We will not rob them of their due, Nor vex the ghosts of other days By naming them along with you.

They sought and found undying fame: They toiled not for reward nor thanks: Their cheeks are hot with honest shame For you, the modern mountebanks!

Who preach of Justice--plead with tears That Love and Mercy should abound - While marking with complacent ears The moaning of some tortured hound:

Who prate of Wisdom--nay, forbear, Lest Wisdom turn on you in wrath, Trampling, with heel that will not spare, The vermin that beset her path!

Go, throng each other's drawing-rooms, Ye idols of a petty clique: Strut your brief hour in borrowed plumes, And make your penny-trumpets squeak.

Deck your dull talk with pilfered shreds Of learning from a nobler time, And oil each other's little heads With mutual Flattery's golden slime:

And when the topmost height ye gain, And stand in Glory's ether clear, And grasp the prize of all your pain - So many hundred pounds a year -

Then let Fame's banner be unfurled! Sing Paeans for a victory won! Ye tapers, that would light the world, And cast a shadow on the Sun -

Who still shall pour His rays sublime, One crystal flood, from East to West, When YE have burned your little time And feebly flickered into rest!